Sketches in Egypt

Sketches in Egypt

C. D. Gibson

Ross & Perry Inc.
Washington, D.C.

No claim to U.S. government work contained throughout this book.

Protected under the Berne Convention. Published 2001

Printed in The United States of America
Ross & Perry, Inc. Publishers
717 Second St., N.E., Suite 200
Washington, D.C. 20002
Telephone (202) 675-8300
Facsimile (202) 675-8400
info@RossPerry.com

SAN 253-8555

Library of Congress Control Number: 2001093108

http://www.GPOreprints.com

ISBN 1-931641-50-1

BRITISH INTELLIGENCE

ILLUSTRATIONS

SKETCHES IN EGYPT
BY
C. D. GIBSON

CHAPTER FIRST

EGYPT has sat for her likeness longer than any other country. Nothing disturbs her composure. Financial ruin may stare her in the face, armies may come and go, but each year the Nile rises and spreads out over her, and all traces of disturbances are gone.

Newspapers may be busy telling of her troubles, but very few of those troubles seem to affect her expression. The stockholders in London worry, and send out more Englishmen to look after their interests.

A Son of the Desert.

Sugar-factories are inspected, and the barrage is doctored. But it is all very quietly done.

The French cabinet may resign on account of her, and the English army may be increased for her sake, but few signs of these compliments does she show. All is tranquil. The only disturbance seems to be made by the dragomans who meet you at the station.

Important events follow each other so closely in Egypt that a year-old guide-book is several chapters too short. Last year it was Kitchener's campaign against the dervishes, and now the French are threatening to interfere with England's march to the Cape. The dragoman is sometimes as satisfactory as the guide-book, and it is often pleasant to find how soon he is through with his recitation and you are allowed to go alone among the great temples. Earthquakes have shaken some in orderly ruin, as if the unseen hands of the men who built them were quietly and slowly building them up again.

But there is a temp-
tation to grow senti-
mental over Egypt.
It is far more cheerful
than it sounds. It is
happy and a place for
a holiday — a country
to make sketches in.
These were made be-
tween December, 1897,
and March, 1898, and
I have been asked to

A Peddler.

help them tell their story of that part of Egypt
the tourist is most likely to see, where the old
and the new world meet most often.

The ancient Egyptian artist must have been
very happy. Temples were built with great
smooth walls for him to cover with pictures
that required very little writing to go with
them, seldom more than Pharaoh's cartouches,
and even these he made more like a picture
than a name. That must have been very

pleasant, and it should have compensated him
for all the restrictions imposed upon him by
the high priest of those days, who often lim-
ited his choice of subject to a king. The
choice of subject is now unlimited. There
never were so many different kinds of people
in Egypt before. But it would be difficult to
draw the king now, for there is much difference of opinion as to who he is.

I left New York with a small library of
Egyptian guide-books, and in nearly every one
of them was a good description of a traveler's
feelings upon arriving at Alexandria or Port
Saïd. I have been in both places, and about
the same sensations will fit either port; and
traveling is too personal a matter to describe
at length, unless it is done with skill. To
give advice is much more simple; and mine
is that if you are on a steamer that is going
through the Canal, don't stay on her until she
gets to Ismailia, but disembark at Port Saïd
and get to Cairo that night all the way by

The Slipper Bazaar, Cairo, January 22, 1898.

Egyptian High Life.

rail. You will see as much of the Canal as you want to, and you will not run the chance of being delayed a day, as the *Königin Luise* was last year by a little tramp steamer that had run foul of a coal-barge.

More advice is to look out of the right-hand window of the car for a first glimpse of the pyramids, the first sure proof that you are in Napoleon's Egypt. After they are once found, it is easy for your eye to follow them through palm-trees and over mud villages until darkness interferes. Then you come to the station in Cairo, a hotbed of porters and dragomans, and through the confusion you finally reach Shepheard's, on the street like a great show-window — all but the plate glass — full of odds and ends from all the world. New arrivals are handed in by the dragomans and porters. It is as if you climbed over the footlights to assist in the performance. You finally stand before the good-looking Mr. Bailer, at the back of the stage. If he thinks you will stand a room overlooking the stable-yard, you will get it. The next morning I moved to the sunny side, overlooking the garden, where a tame pelican walked among tall palm-trees.

The dragoman who first lays hands on you claims you for his own. You will find him waiting for you in the morning. He will sell you antiques, will take you snipe-shooting. He knows when the dervishes will howl or whirl, or where there is a native wedding, to which he will take you. It may be the fame of Shepheard's, or the magic name of Egypt, but it all has a wonderful charm.

The Present Situation.

The remains of Rameses and Seti are lying on their backs out in the Gizeh Museum, and there is a strong desire to hurry to them, in spite of the fact that they will keep. But the panorama in front of Shepheard's is absorbing, and your first morning will most likely be spent in watching it.

A Dealer in Antiquities.

My first afternoon was spent with an evil-eyed dragoman whose pockets were filled with dirty cards and letters, all testimonials from former customers proving that he was, as he continually told me, the best dragoman in the business. He could recite some of

The Bridge.

"Mother Goose," but knew very little English besides.   With him I drove through streets that might have been in Paris, and by barracks and sentries that might have been in London, to a river that could only be

A Village on the Road to the Pyramids.

In the Fish-Market.

in Egypt. My carriage went between the two bronze lions and joined in the procession of camels across the bridge over the famous river to the Gizeh side, where tall trees meet overhead; then to a smaller bridge, more trees, quaint shipping, and a stucco palace, once a harem where some of Ismail's wives lived, and now a museum, the temporary resting-place of those uneasy mummied heads that once wore Egypt's crown; small mouse-

Rameses the Great.

colored donkeys on all sides, and, streaking
in among them, tall camels; then seven
more miles of trees and a good causeway to
the pyramids. Since then I have gone over
the road many times, and I am of the opinion that the Nile's valley would make an
ideal " happy hunting-ground," to which all
good tourists might go when cruel waves
have ceased to toss them and their hotel lives
are over.

All too soon you must go back to Cairo,
where the Bedouin ceases to be the proud
son of the desert and becomes a peddler,
where sheep become mutton and clover is
only fodder. But Cairo is about what the
tourist expects of it and what the hotel pro-
prietor thinks you want. He fills the halls
of his hotel with gaily painted columns, and
on each side of the staircase are gaudy figures; and for those tourists who take their
Egypt between the slipper bazaar and the
fish-market it may do.

At Lady Grenfell's Masquerade Ball—on the eve of Kitchener's
departure for the Soudan.

The Gizeh side of the river is more restful, with its ferry to Bulak, its gardens, and its khedival sporting club, which is Egypt as England would have it— polo twice a week, croquet and rackets, a grand stand, and a steeplechase course ; and the same men who play polo spend their mornings on the desert, teaching their troops to form hollow squares against the day they will have to meet the dervishes.

You should choose your own Cairo. If you leave it to a dragoman you will get mostly howling dervishes and mosques; and if you leave it to a donkey-boy, there is no telling where he will take you — most likely to the fish-market. But with a guide-book and a bicycle you will miss very little that lies between the citadel and the pyramids. Cairo is not all hotel life, and bazaars lining narrow streets like open fireplaces, filled with putty-faced Turks as watchful as the brown buzzards that fly overhead ; there are streets

A Descendant of the Prophet—El Saied Ahmad Abdel
Khalek Affandi, Sheik el Sadat.

that are difficult to find, leading to forgotten
courtyards with great trees standing in the
middle of them, latticed windows bulging out
over uneven pavements below, where black
and gray crows waddle about. In such a

A Bargain in the Ghezireh Gardens.

place sits the neglected Sheik el Sadat, a lineal descendant of the prophet. Through a doorway, in one corner of a tiled room, stands the gold-mounted saddle on which his ancestors once proudly rode. That was long before the days of the Suez Canal, boulevards, stucco palaces, and the opera-house. At court the sheik is no longer the fashion, but there is still a little band of Mohammedans who believe in him. To them the sheik and his old house are sacred. Through the thirty days of Ramadan they sat and howled in his courtyard, and respectfully kissed his hand; and, like the sheik, there must be many other distinguished

A Dancing-Girl.

Oriental relics of the days gone by, left behind by the former tenants, and of no use to the present occupants.

In Egypt the English hold the reins, and one of these days the Egyptian donkey may turn to the left when you meet him, as his distant relative in Whitechapel does. At present he keeps to the right, and staggers along under a load that is much too big for him. To-day he is not the fashion in Cairo. He is only ridden by tourists after dark, through streets that are too narrow and crooked for a carriage. But up the river it is very different. There you learn to like him. From his back you first see Karnak, and the statues of Memnon, and he is forever associated in your memory with the tombs of the kings. Tourists quarrel over him, and in most cases his name is "Rameses, the Great." His chief complaint must be that an Englishman weighs more than an Egyptian; but he should consider

how much better
off the Egyptian is
since the English
have held the reins.
He will only know
of this from his own
observation, and
from what he hears
the English say.
He will never get
it from a French-
man; and the
Egyptian, who
could tell him, is
sulky, and stu-
pidly wishes that
he had been res-

A Daughter of the Nile.

cued by some one else. The half-breed Jew
and Turk in the " Mooskee " is too busy ; and
all the rest of Egypt don't know why they are
better off, or who to thank for law and order
or the improved irrigation that gives them a

fair chance with the rest of civilized mankind. But whether the donkey knows it or not, he is much better off, for an Englishman never rides him when he is old and weak, and that is more than he can expect from his Egyptian friends, who often get on him two at a time.

At Shepheard's people put aside their guide-books for a while. It is a play that requires no libretto. On the crowded piazza overlooking the street, London shopkeepers and foreign noblemen elbow each other, and all celebrities look very much alike.

Cairo is the foyer of Egypt. To go to Egypt and not go up the Nile is very much like standing outside of a theater and watching the audience go in, and then waiting until they come out, to glean from their conversation some idea of the play. But the tourists who go up the river see the drama of Egypt with all its wonderful scenery, and they feel far superior to those who waited for them at

Shepheard's. After one month on the river, it is with a very different feeling they come back to the museum at Gizeh and look on the face of Seti and his distinguished son, whom they have tracked from Sakkara to Philæ and back to their tombs in the sun-baked valley at Thebes, where they had hoped to rest in peace, surrounded by all that a first-class mummy requires during its long wait.

On the Road to Cairo.

CHAPTER SECOND

On the Bank at Komombos.

CHAPTER SECOND

SOME Egypt-bound tourists decide to go up the Nile before they buy their tickets at the company's office in Bowling Green. Others, if they are good sailors, make up their minds before they reach Naples. Some are ill all the way to Port Saïd, and don't care. But most travelers are pretty sure to decide one way or the other soon after Mount Etna

Our Christmas Dinner, Esneh, December 23.

has been left behind, for the East begins
for most people from that moment. If the
guide-books fail to persuade you, there is
pretty sure to be a fellow-passenger who will.
The man who has once seen Upper Egypt
does his best to make you dissatisfied with
Lower Egypt. He can easily show you that
your journey's end is not Cairo, but, at the
very least, the first cataract. This is the
shortest distance he will listen to. And after
he has your promise to go that far, he tells
you of the wonders that can only be seen by
going on to the second cataract.

My fellow-passenger was an old traveler.
Others besides myself fell under the spell
of his eloquence; so, before we had been at
Shepheard's a week, we were a party of six,
with the steam-dahabiyeh *Nitocris* chartered for a month, beginning December 12.
There were growing plants, rugs, and a piano
on her deck, and six state-rooms below. Salem Ghesiri was our dragoman. He spoke

Karnak, January 2, 1898.

good English, and knew the river by heart. Before we left, a few days were spent in buying cork hats and sun umbrellas, and by ten o'clock on the morning of the 12th the crew had unloaded the trucks that had brought our belongings down from Shepheard's, and we had started, with the wind and the current so strong against us that it was all we could do to make six miles an hour against them.

On our left were the mud houses of Old Cairo, with ancient quarries in the distance, and on the right, far beyond a forest of slanting masts that belonged to the picturesque ships which lined the bank, were the tops of the pyramids that we were leaving for a month. As evening approached, the

Salem Ghesiri, Dragoman.

right bank seemed peopled with silhouettes of camels, donkeys, and men, while the figures on the opposite bank were rose-color. To us the day was cool, but to the crew it must have been cold, for their heads were wrapped in shawls and they huddled together in groups about the deck. The awning over us had been removed, and Ali, the pilot, looked like a partly unwrapped mummy as he sat at the wheel.

Those who go up the river in a dahabiyeh like to feel that they are in the same boat with the travelers whose books they read from New York to Port Saïd. This would be a very pleasant feeling, if it did not suggest the responsibility of keeping a record of days that, from all accounts, are sure to be of so much importance. There is a

A Karnak Beggar.

Ali, the Pilot.

sentimental belief that each day on the river is to be of the greatest importance, just as if thousands of tourists on Cook's steamers were not taking the same journey each year. So overpowering becomes this delusion that even letters home seem to take the form of historic biographies, and sound like messages that are sometimes found floating in bottles thrown overboard by shipwrecked people. The Nile itself seems to insist that all mention of it should be made in the form of a diary, for, with very few exceptions, all accounts adopt that mode of expression when they come to it. Cairo and

Statue of Thothmes, Karnak.

Upper Egypt may be treated in the form of essays, but the endless parallel banks of the river immediately suggest that all days will be very much alike and lose their identity, unless they are numbered and described. It seems to be of the greatest importance to find the best way to spell the name of the mud village where you tie up for the night (which name most of the guide-books spell differently)—as if it made any difference to the people at home.

But the diaries on the *Nitocris* during that month were very conscientious and particular about these small things, and I think they will all agree in their spelling, for each one of us waited until all the others had agreed upon the most popular way to spell the names of these various landmarks before we wrote them down.

We soon made friends with our crew. There were sixteen of them. They were

Lunching in Karnak.

An Assiût Donkey.

from every part of Egypt, and of all colors,
shading from the engineer, who was a cream-
colored Turk,—when his face was washed,—
to Ali, who must have been a Sudanese.
Our head steward was almost as black, and
the second steward was another of the cream-
colored variety. We seldom saw the cook.
Sometimes he would put his head and shoul-
ders out of the hatchway, with his arms on
the deck, and then we could see that he was
a little, white-faced Turk with a large black
mustache.

Salem was a Syrian Christian, and he had lost all his earnings in an unprofitable exhibit at the World's Fair in Chicago. His costumes were always elaborate, and he was very ornamental, with his silk sashes and fancy turbans. He superintended our meals, and always suggested the next day's program during dinner; so with our coffee we would read aloud Charles Dudley Warner's and Miss Edwards's opinions of our next stopping-place.

After our first dinner we tied to the bank, by a little village, Salem said, just big enough to have a name. It was dark, and we could hear and see nothing; so we took his word for it.

We were off early the next morning, and all that day the river's banks were fringed with sugar-cane and sakiehs. The many boats we passed were loaded with natives, sometimes perched upon loads of grain, or mixed in with turkeys and cattle.

Temple of Ti.

Tombs of the Kings, Thebes.

On December 14 we made our first landing, and had our first donkey ride, at Beni-
Hassan, one hundred and seventy-one miles
from Cairo.   The Egyptian policemen who
accompanied us to the tombs were out of
keeping with the peaceful look of the place,
and only succeeded in keeping at a distance
the children, who were very pretty.

From the cliffs back of the village we had
our first view of the valley of the Nile, with
its delicate green fields, be-
ginning immediately at the
foot of the sun-baked hills
on which we stood. I rode
back before the rest to
make a sketch ; but the ar-
rival of the post-boat put an
end to that, and its passengers soon had our donkeys,
beggars, naked children,
policemen, and all, and
were taking them back to

A Guardian of the
Temple.

the tombs we had just left. The post-boat
was to us what the foot-prints in the sand
must have been to Robinson Crusoe. Our
frame of mind underwent a change. We
finally became reconciled to the fact that we
were not doing anything uncommon, and
from that moment our diaries suffered. Then
the most contagious of all Nile ambitions
seized us, and our one desire was to find a
mummy.

Most of the 15th was spent with Baedeker,
preparing for Assiût, where we were to tie
up for the night.

After an early breakfast, we climbed the
bank, and found that it was chiefly inhabited
by beggars. We visited the tombs, and
came back to the dahabiyeh by way of the
bazaars, where the natives were dyeing the
dark-blue cloth which they all dress in. That
afternoon we came upon an army of pelicans
on a mud flat in the middle of the river. At
the sound of our whistle they got up, and we

"Most of the day was spent with Baedeker."

lost them far ahead in the twilight, and we thought of that tame pelican that waddles about in Shepheard's stable-yard.

The next day we went by mud villages at the foot of high mountains of white limestone, until we stopped at Farshut for coal, and tried to awaken some sign of friendliness in the natives, who were as dull as the mud banks on which they sat.

On the afternoon of the 18th we reached Keneh, and in fifteen minutes we were on donkeys, going by villages filled with children and barking dogs, on our way to the temple of Dendera. This was to be our first big temple, and Salem had made it his chief excuse for hurrying us away from Beni-Hassan, Assiût, and the rest. Our donkeys raced along the edge of an empty canal, through herds of goats and buffalo, until we saw a low pile of stones in the distance, and then we reached the half-buried temple, and lighted candles, and went down into it and looked up at

the mighty columns. Salem repeated all that
the guide-books knew, and then took us
around to the back wall and showed us the
famous likeness of Cleopatra and her son
Cæsarion.

Salem was pleased with the way we took
our first temple, and rewarded us by saying
it was only the beginning of what was to
come. We complimented him on his choice
of subjects, blew out our candles, picked the
candle-grease from our fingers, and reached
the dahabiyeh by sundown.

By one o'clock, on December 19, we were
abreast of the promised Karnak, and could
see the top of its pylons and obelisk. We
had saved most of our enthusiasm for this
place, and we were anxious to get ashore and
expend it; reluctantly we went by it a few
miles to Luxor for a better landing, where we
were watched by a bank-load of natives until
four o'clock. Then we walked through them
to the village and temple of Luxor, which

Christmas, 1897.

Guardians of the Temple.

served as a curtain-raiser to the next day's visit to the greatest of all temples.

That evening a Cook's steamer arrived, and we were deserted by the crowd on the bank. After dinner Ghesiri entertained the sheiks of the donkey-boys and made arrangements for our mounts for the next day. Two of us volunteered to go to the village and locate the

dancing that the guide-books said could be
found here, but we learned there was to be
none until the following Saturday.

The next day was spent at Karnak, where
Ghesiri led us over its famous stones, until
lunch was brought from the *Nitocris*, and
served in a colonnade surrounded by columns
resembling huge granite lozenges, piled at all
angles, one on top of the other, like ancient
friends, those who had fought successfully
with time supporting those who had been
less fortunate ; and apart from the rest, re-
quiring no support, and with no friends to
be helped, stood the greatest column of them
all, the lonely survivor of the great peristyle
court, with its lotus capital, looking down on
all but its lonely rival, an obelisk. It looks
as though it had been polished and placed
there the day before, in striking contrast to
its unfortunate mate, which centuries ago
gave up battling with earthquakes and wars,
and now lies, a hopeless ruin, at its feet.

Christmas Night—" Auld Lang Syne."

We spent the next three days at Karnak
and Thebes, saving the tombs of the kings
until we should stop again on our way down
from Assuan.

And now the important question was,
Where should we spend Christmas? The
better we knew Karnak and Thebes, the
more forbidding they had grown. They
were too stiff and formal, and their great rigid
Rameses too depressing for a Christmas. We
wanted a cheerful temple, and we found it
at Komombos.

We left Karnak on the morning of December 24, and spent Christmas eve at Edfu.
That night the deck was entirely housed in
by canvas. The crew sat in a circle back of
the smoke-stack, and while they divided the
cigarettes we had bought for them at Luxor,
they listened to our "Down upon the Suwa-
nee River."

Christmas morning we came on deck, and
found that Ghesiri had transformed it into

a bower of palm-branches, sugar-cane, and oranges. The crew were all smiles, and when we presented them with the price of a sheep, they gave us three cheers and a merry Christmas. More cigarettes were distributed, and shortly after breakfast we started for Komombos.

There was little in the day to remind a New-Englander of Christmas. In the lightest clothes, we sat about the deck and watched the villages go by. It was good to see our old friends the water-wheels and cheerful sakiehs again. They looked better to us after our somber stay at Karnak. Early in the afternoon we came to Komombos, the temple we were looking for, and tied to the river's bank just below it; and if you must be traveling on Christmas, there can be no better place to stop.

At Komombos the never-resting Nile has worked its way to the foot of the little hill on which the temple is making its last stand

Thebes, January 2, 1898.

against time. Some kind friends have covered the bank with stones, but the river is slowly wearing them away, and sooner or later it will claim its own; and it will be a pity, for Komombos's temple is dainty in comparison with Karnak, where great stiff Rameses stand with their arms folded across their breasts in very much the same manner in which the real arms are held in the glass case at the Gizeh Museum.

At Karnak there were miles of half-buried walls, and cut deep in them gigantic figures of Rameses, with one hand raised about to strike off the heads of enemies done up in bundles like asparagus and held by the hair of their heads, while armies are shown flying in confusion. The bas-reliefs at Komombos are more cheerful and cut with greater skill. They represent the ancient gods of Egypt in their more playful moods, floating down the Nile, spearing miniature hippopotamuses and crocodiles, with here and there a triumphant procession. The debris of the forgotten city that once covered Komombos has been removed, and the great hall, with its holy of holies now exposed to the light of day, is swept by the wind as clean as a Dutch kitchen; and yet the carvings are as fresh as the day they were made. From the *Nitocris* to the temple is only a few steps through some sugar-cane. It was a novel experience to find no donkey-boys with their patient and sleepy donkeys.

But the natives were different from any we had heretofore seen, and proved that we were getting into real Africa. They were mostly Nubians, and very black, and our preconceived idea of what an African should be.

Komombos and Philæ are the only temples we climbed up to, and it seems to me that they, above all others, lend themselves more readily to the sentimental tourist. It is easier for the imagination to people them; they are more like dwellings.

Some Visitors.

After tea had been brought from the *Nitocris* and served in its portals, we all decided that Komombos would be the temple to own. That evening the crew hung lanterns around the deck among the sugar-canes and palms, and after dinner they gave an exhibition, which started well enough with a dance by the first mate.

Since then I have found that all travelers on the Nile are likely to have this same experience. We were proof against the "Dhabir Devil" that the guide-books had warned us against, but Baedeker had made no mention of the possibility of this entertainment happening to us; still, the crew went at it as though it was an old story with them, and as I write this there may be some unsuspecting tourist about to go through with it. It sounds very good-natured on the part of the crew; and if the entertainment had stopped when the mate had finished the dance, it would have been well enough; but

the dance was only to hold our attention
while the others were getting ready, and
then the dreary horse-play began.   There
was a barber-shop scene, in which flour paste
was used and a door-mat acted as a towel.
A crew that mutinies is tame compared with
an Egyptian crew that acts.   We stopped
them as soon as we could without hurting
their feelings, and they subsided and formed
a circle back of the smoke-stack.   The rest of
the evening was spent in entertainment of our
own choice, and by midnight all was still but
the river, which never rests.

CHAPTER THREE

His Highness Prince Mahomet Ali, Cairo, February 14, 1898.

On the Bank.

CHAPTER THIRD

THE starting of the engines had us up fairly early the next morning, and we found the country very much changed. The desert now came to the river's edge, and granite had taken the place of limestone; it seemed as though we had come to the end of fertile Egypt. Two white vultures were the only living things in sight. Then we

77

came to some wonderful bends in the river,
and the sakiehs once more began to dip up
the muddy water; but the skins of the men
who worked them had changed: they glis-
tened like coal in the sunlight.

By two o'clock we reached Assuan, and
moored to the island of Elephantine, just opposite the town, from which any number of
little bright-painted ferry-boats rowed toward
us; and in a few minutes some thin-legged
Egyptian policemen and a few natives were
on the bank, and a small boy with a stick
had been selected to mind the turkeys that
we had brought from Esneh. Some of the
poor birds were very weak on their legs,
and where they ought to have been red they
were only a pale salmon-color; but the little
cook promised that they would be all right in
a day or two. Some of the crew had homes
on the island, and they all put on their best
clothes and were met by friends. They immediately established a laundry on shore, and

the building of an oven proved that we were
to be there for some time.

We began the 27th with a visit to the
tombs on Grenfell Hill, high on the river's
bank, below Elephantine. There was a
strong wind, full of sand, from the south,
and the light natives had trouble in getting
the heavy boat to the foot of
the hill. The wind helped us
back to the *Nitocris*, and after
lunch we crossed the river to
Assuan, where the inhabitants
seemed especially prepared for
tourists. The natives were
more theatrical in Assuan, and
the bazaars were filled with
musical instruments, made as
primitive as possible to please
the traveler.

There is a railroad at Assuan. It is only a small, dis-
connected link ; but some day

Shopping.

it will be part of a road to the Cape, and vesti-
bule trains will run over it, and passengers
may get only flying glimpses of Philæ from
car windows. Think of being on a train that
went by Pharaoh's Bed in the night! But it
is impossible to believe that the world could
become used to such a wonderful place, and
it is to be hoped that all trains will go slow
when they come to Philæ; for without it
Egypt would be like " Romeo and Juliet"
without a balcony. It is the most romantic
ruin in Egypt, and it marks the end of the
first-cataract tourist's journey.

If the *Nitocris* had been a sailing-daha-
biyeh, and had belonged to us, and if the season had been younger and the river higher,
we would have had her pulled up one cataract after another until we had made some
important discoveries; but we were one-
month tourists on a hired boat, and that
night, while the *Nitocris* was tied fast to
some large wooden pegs driven deep into the

Shepheard's Hotel, Cairo.

A Luxor Dancing-girl.

beach, we read how the *Rip Van Winkle* and other dahabiyehs had gone to Abu-Simbel.

The next morning we chose the nine-o'clock train, in preference to camels and donkeys; and after some minutes of rocking and twisting in the little box-car, we were ferried from the mainland to the famous island, where we were to forget Komombos and all the others amid new beauties, which no guide-book can exaggerate.

After lunch we walked to the northern end of the island, boarded a big, clumsy, eight-oared boat with a great deal of rigging lashed overhead, and our homeward journey began. There was a crew of ten, and we soon had the greatest respect for their skill, especially one little man with crooked teeth, who sat in the stern and shouted over our heads at the men in the boat.

The rapids were tame enough at first. The wind was strong against us, and we found some shelter behind the high granite islands we drifted among. The river had worn them into fantastic shapes so closely resembling temples that hieroglyphics had been cut on the polished stones by the Pharaohs, who never tired of seeing their names in print.

At one place we stopped and watched ten or fifteen boys swim and float down a part of the rapids. They would come shivering up to us, and the next instant they would be in

Camel-back.

the water shooting by us on a log, scream-
ing to attract our attention, and then back
again to us, with their teeth chattering for
bakshish.

But after that it was very different. The
man at the tiller half stood up, and I could
see, by the little patches of sand on his fore-
head that the wrinkles there had formed in
two parallel lines, that he had been praying
while we had been watching the boys swim,
and by the same sign I could see that most
of the crew had been doing the same thing;
and Mohammed must have been with us, for
fifty times within half that number of minutes
we needed help. With the little man in the
stern continually wetting his lips and jamming
the tiller from side to side, apparently steer-
ing in just the wrong place, and always proving that he was right, we " shot " over the
uneven surface of the river, dodging half-
buried rocks, first near one bank and then the
other, until we reached the natural bed of the

The Sheik of the Pyramids.

river.   Here the crew began their battle with the wind, and by evening, after much chanting and hard rowing on their part, we reached the *Nitocris*, feeling very much as if our faces had been sandpapered.

During our stay at Elephantine we made friends with four little Bisharin girls.   They were graceful and pretty, and had the power to make the most dismal tomb cheerful. They followed us to the quarries back of Assuan, and turned the top of the half-finished obelisk into a stage and danced in the sunlight, while the blackest man in Africa played an instrument of his own invention. And the last I remember of Assuan is their

On Grenfell Hill.   The Keeper of the Tomb,
Assuan, December 29, 1897.

four little figures wrapped in the brightest-colored shawls that could be bought in Lower Egypt, and they waving their hands until a bend in the river hid them.

It was a novelty to find ourselves going with the current, which had been until now against us, and we could count on much bigger runs; but there was double the danger of running on a sand-bar, and from that time on there was always a man with a pole in the bow.

On the 30th we stopped beneath our old friend Komombos, and visited Edfu the next day; and from the top of its pylons we looked into the mud-walled yards of the town, where little fly-covered children stopped playing with goats and called to us, even at that height, for bakshish.

On the 31st we were once more in Luxor, where the donkey-boys and beggars gave us a hearty welcome. Again we visited Thebes, and were followed from tomb to tomb by the usual venders of imitation antiques and shriveled mummy-hands.

Our trips back from Thebes were always enlivened by donkey-races across the great fields of young wheat, in the middle of which the great Memnons sit. Those races generally proved that "Columbus" was a faster donkey than "New York."

Pharaoh must have continually thought of the future. His tombs at Thebes show how anxious he was to outlast time. And it seems hard that his carefully prepared plans should have been interfered with. How impressive it would be to find, at the end of the long subterranean passage, the king whose one wish had been to lie there. He must have visited it often before his death. He might have superintended its building and criticized the drawings that decorate its walls. But the sarcophagus is now empty, and its lid is broken, and the king's new friends have put him in a cheap wooden house; and written

At the Races, Khedival Sporting Club.

on a piece of cardboard, and
tacked on the glass case in
which he now lies, is the
name he was so fond of cut-
ting in granite.

An Assuan Beggar.

One year more or less
makes very little difference
to Egypt, but the New
Year was properly welcomed
aboard the *Nitocris*, for one
of us had never seen a January 1 before. So it happened
that, even in Egypt, the occasion was treated
as a novelty, and the *Nitocris* once more
blossomed out with lanterns, and looked as
well that night as her more graceful rivals,
the sailing-dahabiyehs, that were anchored
above and below us.

January 4 was our last day at Luxor.
We had ridden up the limestone valley at
Thebes to the tombs of the kings, had spent
several days and a moonlight night at Kar-

nak. We had said good-by to our donkey-
boys. Mine had held an umbrella over me
with one hand and had fought natives at the
same time with the other, and I hope that
some day he will be a dragoman. Before
daylight on the 5th we had once more
started north, with only five more days on
the river left to us. At night we tied to
the bank and walked through moon-lighted
villages, and did our best to imagine that our
journey had only just begun.

On the evening of the 7th an extraordi-
nary thing happened. It rained hard enough
to make a noise on the awning over us, and
in the excitement we almost forgot that there
were only three more days between us and
Cairo. We had begun to count the hours
and to dread that fatal bend in the river that
would show us the pyramids at Sakkara,
where we were to spend our last night. We
passed dahabiyehs with American and English
flags flying over them, and we were filled with

An Artist in the Mouskie.

envy. Handkerchiefs and parasols were sympathetically waved at us, and at a distance we may have looked cheerful; but it was a forlorn, childish feeling to be taken home because our time was up and our dahabiyeh had another engagement. We felt that all the other boats knew our secret, and we even suspected the crew of having become tired of us and only remaining civil in order to collect the present that they were expecting.

Ghesiri's suggestion that we spend the night of the 10th at Cairo seemed to prove that they were anxious to have done with us; but we had no inclination to be tied to the bank at Cairo overnight, waiting to be sent away in the morning before a crowd of natives, and among them, possibly, those other people who had chartered our boat. We would wait at Sakkara, and not get to Cairo one minute before our time was up.

On the 8th we visited a sugar-factory at

Our Bisharin Friends, Assuan.

Tel-el-Amarna, and later on the same day passed our first landing-place, Beni-Hassan.

By noon on the 9th we reached the fatal bend in the river and saw that we were once more in the land of pyramids, and we were soon tied to the bank beneath which once stood the city of Memphis.

We rode to Mariette's House, past the pyramids and the colossal Rameses lying on his back among tall palms, surrounded, for some reason, by a mud house, as if the great granite figure had not already proved that it could continue its battle with time unassisted by a few mud bricks and some tin roofing that is very much in the way.

We lighted candles and walked through the hot, suffocating galleries of the mausoleum, and peered into the huge granite sarcophagi that once held the mummied sacred bulls. Then we rode to the tomb of Ti, and Ghesiri's last lecture was about that gentleman.

Beni-Hassan.

In the distance was Cairo; and even a view of the pyramids at Gizeh and the citadel failed to console us, and we still mourned our late month on the Nile. We took our last donkey-ride through the palms that now grow where Memphis once stood, and reached the *Nitocris* by sundown.

By midday on the 10th, we shook hands with the crew and left the *Nitocris* tied to the bank where we had first found her, just as though nothing had happened; and, after all, what had happened was this: six more tourists had gone to the first cataract and back, and a few more Egyptian sketches had been made. For us the performance of the Nile was at an end, and we were once more in the streets on our way to the Gehzireh Hotel, with a determination to console ourselves with Cairo, which now looked to us, after our stay in the country, like a full-grown European capital.

By January 10 the season had commenced

At Philæ.

and the prices of rooms had doubled. Since
we left, several steamers from the west had
brought an army of tourists, who were turn-
ing Africa into New York, London, and
Paris. And at the Casino, in the Ghezireh
Gardens, was as good an imitation of Monte
Carlo as the law allows, but such a poor
one that even the Frenchmen who worked it
seemed ashamed of themselves, and the New-
Yorker who owned it was very seldom seen
there.

"As good an imitation of Monte Carlo as the law allows."

At Shepheard's there is always the man
who has "been there before," and like the
same man at the play, he sits beside you and
interprets the picture. You finally promise
that you will not go to the *mouskie* without him, and that you will not see the Sphinx
by moonlight unless he is there; for if you
do, not having been there before, you will be
sure to go too early or too late. He says
the moon should be at just such an angle
and no other. The peddlers in the mouskie
know him, and while they entertain him with
little cups of sweet tea they complain that
they have had no luck since they last saw
him, and they ask eagerly after that gentleman he brought to them the year before — the
gentleman who had such exquisite taste and
backed it up so generously with his money.
And you drink their tea, and feel, as you
leave the shops, after having only looked at
their things, that they will never ask affec-
tionately after you. The man who has been

there before generally walks in front of you, as if he were not as anxious to have you see the place as he is to have you see that he knows his way about; and, after all, it is no small thing to be proud of. If I ever go to the mouskie again, I shall pity the green-horn who happens to be with me.

The bazaars are dirty, and so many pasty-faced Turks squatting about in the filth grow tiresome. At first they are described in letters home as fascinating and picturesque, and whole days are spent with them, buying hundreds of things that are destined to be left in hotel bureau drawers and gradually lost. The souvenirs we buy in the mous-kie seem to melt away. The precious stones we bought there turn to glass, the slippers become pasteboard, the gilt things tarnish, and the brass-work bends itself into old junk, and the mouskie is only a confused dream; so no wonder the old trav-eler is proud that he can actually find his

"The man who has ' been there before.' "

In a Coffee-house, Cairo.

way about in it.   He had probably begun
to think that there never had been such a
place.

But Egypt is full of real things, and probably the most genuine thing of them all is
the English occupation.   Egypt herself is the
best proof of how necessary to her well-be-
ing this is.   It is hard to tell just how un-
happy the fellaheen were before the English

came. The Egyptian is not the sort of man
that complains. After centuries of oppres-
sion, he now accepts whatever form of government is offered in a browbeaten way, and
shuffles along after his donkey, and pays his
tax for bringing a few bundles of clover
across the bridge into Cairo without a mur-
mur; and, judging by his looks, I doubt if
he would make much disturbance if he found,
some morning, that the tax on his clover
had been doubled. He evidently feels like a
very small depositor in a broken bank. England is the largest creditor, and is straight-
ening things out for them both, and he is
satisfied.

There never were so many cooks trying to
spoil a broth. Before a consul-general is re-
ceived by the Khedive, the Sultan of Turkey
must first approve of him, and it is said that
the Sultan allows months to go by before he
gives his consent, which is his Oriental way
of showing his authority. But Egypt is

geographically so important that, in spite of
herself, she will be saved, and with England's
help she will some day pay her debts, and in
centuries to come the fellah may learn to hold
his head up like the Nubian.

There is no fear of Egypt becoming dull
and commonplace, for if the East and the
West should ever fight, it must be for the
possession of her canal; and many an unborn
soldier's reputation will be made before the
railroad that has started up the Nile's valley
reaches Cape Town. The same land that
offers death and reputation to the strong
gives life to the weak, and the tired rich
man on his dahabiyeh and the soldier on the
transport go up the Nile side by side, and in
most cases they both find what they are in
search of.

Shepheard's, in all probability, will forever remain a composite portrait of Europe
and Asia, with Cairo as its frame. Time has
made, and probably will continue to make,

some slight alteration in Upper Egypt's appearance ; but the locomotive's whistle will have difficulty in breaking the silence and calm of Karnak and Thebes. And the present indications are that Egypt will remain true to the Pharaohs of old, and until the judgment-day she will, in all probability (assisted by the Nile, who made her), continue to quietly resist the attentions of modern nations, and patiently wait for that last day.

At Komombos.

www.ingramcontent.com/pod-product-compliance
Lightning Source LLC
Chambersburg PA
CBHW021340090426
42742CB00008B/672